EFFECTIVE MARKETING WITH
SOCIAL MEDIA

Leveraging Social Media as a tool for powerful marketing that leads to increase in sales and loyal consumer base.

Table of Contents

INTRODUCTION 4
SOCIAL MEDIA MARKETING 6
ESSENTIALS OF SOCIAL MEDIA MARKETING 7
    SET ATTAINABLE GOALS 7
    KNOW YOUR TARGET 8
    BE ON RELEVANT PLATFORMS 9
    IT'S NOT ALL ABOUT SALES 9
AGE GROUPS AND SOCIAL MEDIA MARKETING 10
    Baby Boomers 10
    Generation X 10
    Millennials 11
    iGeneration 12
CREATING POWERFUL CONTENTS 13
    Humorous content 13
    Emotional Content 14
    Rational Content 15
    Event and Seasonal Contents 16
    Educative content 16
    Interactive Contents 16
UTILIZING SOCIAL MEDIA PLATFORMS 18
    FACEBOOK 18
    YouTube 22
    TikTok 24
    Quora 27
    Pinterest 28

 Messenger 31

Tips and Tricks of SMM 33

 Use Paid Ads 33

 Boost High-Performing Contents 33

 Test Ads 33

 Post When the Audience is Online 34

 Courtesy is Key 34

 Give Discounts and Giveaways 34

 Cross-Promote 34

 Invest in a website 35

 Always Sell 35

 Be Patient 35

CONCLUSION 36

INTRODUCTION

Every day, people try to connect with their families and loved ones. The young and old from different cultures, communities, and diverse beliefs all connect on social media. Businesses try to get their goods or services out there to people every day, exploiting mediums they know that work. Now is not the day to pick up the phone and make cold calls nor the days to use TV and radio advertising. This is because there is a more efficient and cheaper method of getting your products and services out to the world – using social media.

With social distancing becoming the days' norm, you have to get your goods or service to the world without getting in touch physically with the outside world. Fortunately, just as if we've been prepared for this, social media has proved to be the best way to create awareness for your business. You just asked how social media is that powerful? Let's find out.

As at the time of this writing, it has been estimated that about 3.8 billion people use social media[1]. Among this 3.8 billion people are your potential customers. To get to them, you need to know how best you can utilize these social media platforms. With people spending around an average of five hours online, there is no better place to target your consumers. Even ads on social media platforms are cheaper and target your customers three times better than television and radio ads. Isn't that great? I'd say, "Dispose conventional advertising."

There are several social media platforms that you can use to promote your business effectively. Name any popular social media platform and you are really on point. Facebook, Twitter, Quora, Pinterest, and even the replica for TV, YouTube are very good platforms that can be converted to very powerful and effective media of marketing that will give your business the boost you've been wanting.

Even the new social media platform, TikTok, has been performing excellently in helping big brands and even small businesses to market their products and services. All social media platforms are very powerful tools that can be leveraged, with the right education, to make business' revenue hit the sky. So, I think we have to say bye to very expensive marketing platforms and strategies as social media beats and even outperforms most of them and eventually keeps you smiling.

---

[1] **Source:** WeAreSocial and Hootsuite's 2020 Global Overview Report

With the right information on social media marketing, you will able to meet your target consumers, within a target location. With the right steps, you can use this powerful tool to increase your sale as you will promote your business in a very efficient and low-cost way. This seems like some super-easy plan, right? No, it's not. Most of the small businesses that try to implement social media marketing fail because they don't have enough knowledge to make it a success. Also, most fail because they are not consistent with what they are doing and others fail because they fail to implement what they have done at the right time.

Fortunately for you, you are currently reading the richest social media marketing information that's worth above $5000 in consultation. You have all you need to wield social media into your revenue generator. Having this book isn't all about reading the book and saying 'Yeah! I did it.' It is about doing everything, step by step, all that is written in this book where and when required. Even if you are just opening an account on one of the social media platforms and you are still just finding your way around, with this eBook, you will have enough information to get things fixed real quick and be on the top of your marketing game.

In this eBook, you will be taught how to leverage social media tools to produce a very powerful promotion that will bring you an increase in consumer base which in return will lead to an increase in sales! It doesn't end there. You will know what to do to convert these buyers to returning customers that will later become loyalists! Look forward to that!

PS: I recommend that you check out important links attached to this eBook for better understanding. It's a very good plus for the knowledge.

SOCIAL MEDIA MARKETING

How can we define this powerful tool? We can say that social media marketing is the act of using social media platforms as tools to connect with potential customers and also building brand awareness simultaneously. Using social media marketing is communicating with your customers in a way that makes them feel attached and belonged to your brand which in the long run will bring about an increase in sales.

Currently, there is no other efficient way to promote your products and services to the world since there is now a strict restriction hindering physical contacting – social distancing. Hearing this seems like the end of the road for a lot of business owners but that does not mean you have to fold your business and cry alone in your bed. No. Social media marketing is your hero. It has always been around to utilize but you need it more now than before.

In 2016, Poo-Pourri, a company that sells odor-eliminating toilet-spray debuted their ad video on their Facebook page and ended up selling over 20 million bottles using social media as primary advertisement media. Inarguably, their marketing strategy was solid enough to bring about that much of a sale. This is an example of how advantageous social media can be to businesses. Social media's marketing potential can be exploited effectively when you know what to do, where, and when.

Social media marketing is not all about getting your products sold alone, it does well to help you add value to customers and even engage them in conversations. You get to know what your customers are saying and how they feel about your product, service, or brand. The feedback you receive from your customers on social media is quite important and you can use this to enhance your social media marketing, targeting your customers appropriately.

There is nothing as good as expanding your consumer base exponentially. Having loyal customers provides your business with ready customers for new products and services. Loyal customers also increase your customer base through recommendations.

Before launching or deciding to engage in social media marketing, there are several things you need to know and consider that will help you succeed. These things are mentioned in the next chapter. Let's dive right into it!

ESSENTIALS OF SOCIAL MEDIA MARKETING

Before you launch an ad campaign on any social network of your choice or create content to post on your social media account, there are certain guidelines to guide you as you go about them to do them aright and making your overall strategy work out well. This information is the one that differentiates the successful campaign from the unsuccessful ones.

Here, we will discuss some important considerations in social media marketing. This consideration applies to all social media platforms that would be discussed and need to be thoroughly ironed out to bring about a very-effective social media marketing strategy.

SET ATTAINABLE GOALS

Before you start creating an account for your business on a social media platform, you need to ask yourself and find out what your goal is. You need to think well and ask yourself why you are about to kick start your social media marketing plan. There might be several goals, agreed, but there is usually an ultimate goal as to why you are doing what you are doing.

Also, don't set unrealistic goals. For a new business, making over 20 million sales in 3 months might not be realistic enough. Setting a realistic goal will keep pumping your zeal fuel and keep you going. Doing the opposite will make you frustrated even before you are mid-way into your social media marketing strategy.

Your social media marketing goal will be the solid foundation on which you build your overall strategy. Yours might be to increase your brand awareness, drive traffic to your website, or just increase your sales by a certain percentage. A defined and attainable social media marketing aim will help you to set objectives that align and brings about a satisfactory end. You will enjoy every bit of the process as all you will be doing will continue to advance towards a set goal.

If you have a set goal before, now would be a good time to revisit that goal and see if it is attainable. There is room for changes if it doesn't align with 'feasible'. Restructure and readjust where necessary. It's going to get better from there.

Also, set a time for a befitting goal. I used befitting because it's not all goals that can be dated. For instance, when the goal is to provide customer support and it is dated, there is seen to be a misconception. But reaching ten thousand followers on twitter in the next year seems more possible than the former.

The importance of dating your goals cannot be underestimated. With the date in mind, you will be challenged to make your aim true before the set time. It will create as self-awareness and prompt you to do all you can not to miss that deadline. Also, do all you can to stay aware of that date. Except if you are working for someone, you are the only one to evaluate your performance and if you fail, you will solely bear the consequences. So, keep yourself always in check, making sure that your activities align with your set goal.

KNOW YOUR TARGET

Ken runs a business that sells luxury watches. He was determined to make his business grow within a year and decided to launch a massive ad campaign on Facebook. Of course, this is a good business decision and could make his dream come true. But he decided to run the Facebook ad campaign all by himself, believing there is no big deal about it. His ad was sincerely catchy and he targeted his ad to everyone from 18 years of age in his country.

This seemed like a good target, maybe. Well, after a week of running the ad campaign, he just had only 3 orders compared to tens he had expected. Unfortunately, the campaign failed. Why? His content was okay. The ad was catchy and quite engaging but his targeting was wrong. "Targeting".

You know who your frequent customers are. You can guess their age group and classify them accordingly. Targeting a bicycle ad to older age groups is very probable to be unsuccessful as most of them will prefer other transportation means to cycling.

On social media, no matter how good your content or your ad is, when you serve the wrong audience with your content or advertisement, it's just like serving the salad on tea. Wrong! Your target audience is clusters of age groups that you need to know.

Even as a new business, you should be able to point to a specific age group as your target customer. You shouldn't believe that you cater for everyone. Even if you sell food products, some age groups are dominating in buying your goods. They are decision-makers or influence household decisions. You have to be able to identify your target and address your content and ads to them accordingly.

This will save you from extra costs. An exhaustive introduction to this age group is in a whole chapter after this. So, don't worry about not knowing which is which.

BE ON RELEVANT PLATFORMS

While it is not bad to have an account on all the popular social media platforms, it is more effective if you major on specific ones that relate to your business. This will make you focus on important channels that relatively target your possible customers. Remember everyone's preference for social media platforms is different, so you might want to consider ones that most of your possible customers are on.

For someone offering photography service, YouTube is not the right platform for such a person. Twitter might be a bit odd too. Using Instagram and Pinterest might be the most effective method of getting to potential customers as both platforms accommodate pictures more than the aforementioned. So, you must diligently select the platforms that will suit your business goals and make your expectation a reality. Also, remember to be dedicated to a few and not all.

IT'S NOT ALL ABOUT SALES

When using social media for marketing, you are directly connecting with people in a place that they just want to communicate and have fun. Using social media might have the main aim of increasing revenue but adding value and communicating comes first. No business wants a one-time client. A way to build a loyal fan base for your business is using social media if and only if you don't make it all about yourself but about the people you are targeting on whichever platform you chose to promote on.

Gradually creating credibility and building impression that will last for a long time will get you continuous sales. A social media platform is not a marketplace where people just have to buy what you have to offer. You should communicate with them and also add value to them. That is one sure way to increase your prospective customer and also sales, eventually.

Knowing who your customers are matters. It is worth a chapter discussing them. So, you have it!

AGE GROUPS AND SOCIAL MEDIA MARKETING

Consumers' age matters, after location, when social media promotion is to be brought to the table. In recent years, there is an improvement in the adverts and promotions strategy as they are mainly targeted towards specific age groups. It is imperative to note that different marketing strategies are applied to different age groups.

Whether they are young and exploring or old and conservative, you have to be able to direct to them the right content that will engage them and eventually turn them to be your loyal customers. Loyal customers are five times liable to buy from the brand they are loyal to. So, it would be an advantage if you target the right age groups on social media. Let's see who they are.

Baby Boomers

People belonging to this age group are people from 55 to 73 years old. They consist of old people that still engage in transactions and societal norms. These people are quite the loyal type and can be bought with very informative content. However, they are very loyal to a business once they find it satisfying.

A major factor that should be highly considered is that these age groups are focused on accuracy in detail. They make all the findings they can before they buy from you. They check reviews and star ratings of products and services. So, ensure that information is easily available on the internet, preferably on popular review websites and also yours.

These people want to be seen as special. So, it would benefit you if you engage them often. If using your product or service is very complex, then you should find a way to simplify it if they are your target customer. Putting up posts on usage guides might work well for these age groups.

Generation X

Generation X are people within the age group of 39 to 54 years old. They are majorly parents that are strong decision-makers in their household or leaders in their respective industries. This age group is highly targeted by major businesses because of their decision making characteristics. People in this age group influence the decisions of younger age groups greatly and also influences the baby boomers slightly. What they want is a summary but clear information on your product or services.

Generation X are mobile phone users but are related to the baby boomers with the tablet and desktop computer usage. The composure of this generation loves the usage of tablets and desktops better but those that do not use this can have a smartphone or have it as a supplement for tabs and desktops. In order of domination, Facebook, YouTube, Instagram, LinkedIn, and Pinterest are social media platforms that these age groups dominate. Your social media platform will depend on your convenience and type of content you will be posting regularly.

Generation X is interested in video content. They are huge fans of YouTube. However, keeping it short and quite simply is the magic to getting the attraction of this age group. You would want to be brief and concise with your video posts if you are targeting this age group.

Millennials

Those within the age range of 23 to 38 are those that are in this age group. This age group is a heavy user of the internet. Their presence is significant on all social media platforms and can be the center of focus on most of them. They dominate Facebook, Instagram, TikTok, Twitter, and even YouTube! They are virtually everywhere.

They are lovers of trends and are quite flexible in joining any trend at any time. They love 'fast and trends' They would buy from any brand that is trending anytime. They easily switch to other brands too but the rate decreases as they increase in age. Millennials like trying out new things. This age group likes catchy things and can be attracted to catchy post headlines, subjects, pictures, and videos.

You should always try to stir the curiosity of this age group to find out more about your business or a product. Ensure your posts and ads are short, catchy, and concise when targeting this age group. They are fans of video content but would only be interested if it's with a catchy topic, and also short. Photos are of great attraction to them too. They are good researchers too and would more likely try to find out about your business or the service it offers before settling for it.

Asides the things mentioned, another way to get this age group's attention is by offering promo and discounts. They are lovers of promotional content and would engage with one when they find it.

The best part of this age group is that they easily fall in love with short, emotional content. They are quite emotional and would always want to know how people that have used the product felt. They would want to know how attached your loyal fan base is and the link of attachment. This information, when gathered, will more likely make them decide about your business and its products or services.

iGeneration

The smallest cohort of internet users are people within this age group. They are people who are younger than 23 years of age. Almost all the time, they are not in the decision-making class, and their decisions are influenced or made by Millennials and Generation X age group.

If your product can be used by people in this age group, you can easily influence them to have a strong affinity for your product. This may last for a long time because they, most times than often, stick to a product they love.

For this age group, short and humorous content is the best for them. Making it a cartoonish for very young ones is a good plus too. They would love to see someone their age gives a short, interesting song or some little tricks that are, of course, related to your business or product. These age groups can be quite engaging if you serve them with the right content. Serve them with short and simple instructional pictures or videos on how to use your product. Also, include a 'why' then you have their attention.

Note that they will more likely be showing your content to an adult parent or guardian. So, be prepared to create a balance in gaining the interest of both age groups. However, ensure that the ad or post buys the interest of these children more. The can be quite adamant when their attention has been caught.

The importance of targeting gender is also very huge to be unconsidered. Some products target women and some are targeted towards men. Some are for mums and some products for a woman expecting a baby. So, as you are considering age groups, consider the gender too.

CREATING POWERFUL CONTENTS

Selecting random content to post fails 99% of times than when you strategically select your content to the perfect target audience. It might seem simple, of course. Pick a picture or video, add a heading, add some bit of info then post or publish the ad. It seems that simple. Yes, it is! But you have to be endowed with the right information on how to present your content and create an engaging ad to place it in the top 1%.

Each cohort of target customers needs a different type of content. Although some might be effective in most of the age groups, there are specific contents targeted for specific businesses and at a specific time. An advert with father Christmas is not ideal during any time of the year besides December. Creating an animation for an automobile advertisement is wrong because, one, you are targeting a mature age group and two, that is just so wrong!

Understanding how each content works will give you a deep understanding of how to make the right targeting for the optimal result. Knowing what works and why will help you in selecting the right content at the right time. The different content types are quite powerful when used effectively. Let's check out some of the most powerful content and how we can put them to good use.

Humorous content

Writing jokes is never easy. But if you have a rich humor gist, then you can trust your marketing campaign. Laughter is universal. Everyone would possibly laugh or smile at a piece of humor seen on the internet. You can imagine why memes and witty hashtags quickly became popular. You can successfully make your content viral if you include good humor.

First, funny content gets shared quickly on social media. I'm sure you've noticed the trend also. People will keep sharing until it becomes viral. Associating your customers with your business using humor is smart. Besides using humor to get them to relax, it also makes them 'feel good' about you.

How do you write humorous marketing content? First, let's exclude marketing content and talk about funny. How do you write 'humor'? Humor is a sweet spot between offensive and every day. Being funny is between offensive and benign. For instance, right-clicking your mouse is an everyday thing that isn't funny. Also, rejecting insults from your boss is a violation – an offensive isn't funny. Right-clicking on your mouse to reject your boss' insult sounds funny, right? That's humor.

There are various ways you can post very humorous content that will be shared by your social media followers. However, be sure that your content doesn't seem offensive to some people. Making a joke about a pet might be fine until someone accuses you of something you are not even thinking about while making the joke. As a big brand or small business owner, you have to do a lot of testing before you post your content or uploading that meme you've made. I would advise that you ask some of your friends what they think about your already-made humorous content. Send to people you are sure would give an honest review before posting.

Humorous content can get the job done with the right application. Someone crying and feeling frustrated a few minutes ago might be laughing so hard in a few minutes because of a simple line of a joke. There, you create an impression that will last for a very long time.

There is no time of the year that you can't mix a few words to make a joke. However, short and smart should not be left out.

Emotional Content

About seven years ago, I saw Dove's Real Beauty Sketches campaign video. I'm not a campaign video fan, but I still saw till the very end! Another thing is that I still remember that video to this day! Why? It got me emotionally attached. I'm sure there is a high probability of remembering a tragic movie you saw some years ago that made you cry or a very funny movie that you saw when you were younger. Mr. Bean?

Let's say you saw two ads of new businesses which happen to follow each other on your social media account. You decided to check both out and decide where to buy based on what you see. One of the ads talked well about the product and the other got you emotionally attached so deeply that you cried. Which one do you think would 'impress' you enough to buy? The one that made you cry, right?

Emotion is natural to man. We can't but feel emotional. The first ad instance above is not bad, is it? It's not. But the other ad stands out because it connects with your emotion and gave a good first impression. There is a very high probability that you will buy from the business with the other ad because there, you are buying with your heart. This is just what emotional marketing does – makes people buy with their hearts.

Not forgetting to mention, video is the best tool for emotional content. Pictures follow. The videos must be communicating with the viewers and make them feel loved and cared for. Remember it is all about them. Emotional attachment will make new customers connect strongly with your brand. Affinity is sure if you do just what's right.

Also, Target just one emotion of your customer. Don't mix happy and sad emotions. Be precise. If you are creating a happy content, don't add a bit of anger into it. That's unfair. Be definite, pass the message, aim for a feeling, and do all that in the shortest time you can.

Ultimately, you can pass just a message using several emotional contents. Dove, for instance, passes the message 'every woman is beautiful' using very strong emotional content. If your tagline is 'Every man is a King', for example, you can pass that sole message using several emotional contents.

Telling a story is also a surefire way you can connect with the audience. Whatever the emotion you are using to connect, you can still connect with the audience of any age group. Proctor & Gamble, whose target consumers are mothers, told a story with their "Thank You Mom" commercial where famous Olympians were featured to tell stories of how their moms supported their careers. They told compelling stories and market their products at the same time.

A quick add: A study made by Psychologytoday.com shows that emotional content performed two times better than rational contents among 1400 evaluated advertising campaigns that were successful.

Rational Content

The name defines it – Rational. This includes descriptive or informative content. You can't always be funny or emotional. You should get some facts out there too. Let people know about your product or service but in an appealing manner. Let them know the business is not all about you and selling your products. Let them know that it's about them and that they are cared for while passing the message at the same time. Need a hint? 'We thought about you and designed XYZ to make your every day easier. It's been designed with ABC to... .'

Event and Seasonal Contents

Expectedly, some products are suitable for certain seasons and services for a specific time of the year. The same goes for the contents you post during the year. Investing heavily in an odd[2] emotional marketing campaigns sometimes around December might not be the best timing even if your content is good. Everyone is excited in December you shouldn't make them sad or angry.

Also, when a big event is upcoming, you can use it as a motivation for your advert. When an event like the World cup is upcoming, you can use the theme for your marketing campaign. This might be effective if you are targeting men in your business as they make up a large number of soccer fans. Based on the selective marketing style, the timing for special events and seasons might be just on point, considering your audience composition. Seasonal content should be planned ahead of time to bear an effective result.

Educative content

As a business owner looking to be successful on social media, you must be able to add value to your audience. Let your posts not be about you alone, include their interest too. Does your business sell cake ingredients? Teach them how to bake a cake on video using your ingredients. Your audience will want to try out what you have taught using the precise tools and ingredients – which includes yours! You can even engage them to make the cake themselves and share the pictures for you to post on your page.

Educating your audience will make them stick to you as they will be actively commenting and asking questions for them to make it right. This will give them a feeling that you care about them and that your product simply just adds value to them.

Interactive Contents

In 2018, posts with questions were seen to be the second-best most engaging content after videos. Interactive posts are like wildfire. Spreading and causing excitement. When you ask your audience a direct question, you are simply telling them that you care about their opinions. Ensure you reply to every comment especially when you are a new business. As expected, you might not be able to

---

[2] Odd in this definition is an emotion that doesn't get you excited.

reply to everyone later on but do well to reply to a few when your fan base grows. An instance is a sportswear business asking a simple question "When is your next run?"

You can also organize competitions with one of your products as a prize. Ensure the competition is quite fun and easy to do without buying anything expensive. Also, you can ask your audience to choose for you or themselves. You might also engage people by asking them to vote, share a picture, or tell a story. Interactive content will create that customer-to-business relationship that your business needs to thrive.

UTILIZING SOCIAL MEDIA PLATFORMS

Why choose Facebook for your business? Why not Instagram? Have you ever considered YouTube? Sometimes, we are confused about choosing the platform to use for promoting our businesses. One might be thorn between one's interest and business requirement. You might love Instagram but your business might not be the type you can promote on the same social media platform.

It is guessable that you are feeling pumped up about launching that social media marketing strategy. But you need to find out some information on the social media you are targeting. If you are trying to widen your audience, targeting the Millenials for example, you have to ensure that they are participating on that social media platform you are considering.

Here, some very popular social media platforms are going to be considered for you to choose from. You can easily identify the best platform(s) that will befit your business to cause an eventual increase in revenue and create massive awareness for your business. There are statistical facts, which includes demographic data, on each social media platform accumulated from reliable sources to help you make the best marketing decisions. This is because data is very important for any marketing strategy starting from selecting the best platform to deploying a marketing strategy.

FACEBOOK

Facebook has been operational for over 15 years and it has been ranked the second most used social media platform. It is quite popular and is constantly increasing its members monthly. It is the global village that everyone has a spot on.

In the United States, adults are the ones dominating the said platform. They are most frequent on this platform, visiting at least once a day. The teens, however, are leaving this platform for other teen-buzzing platforms like TikTok. However, using Facebook for marketing is still quite effective for youths and adults likewise.

Let's check out some statistics. A recent study made by **Pew Research** shows that 60% of adults in the US use Facebook and among those who use Facebook, 74% visit the social media platform at least once a day. Even Instagram doesn't beat this number.

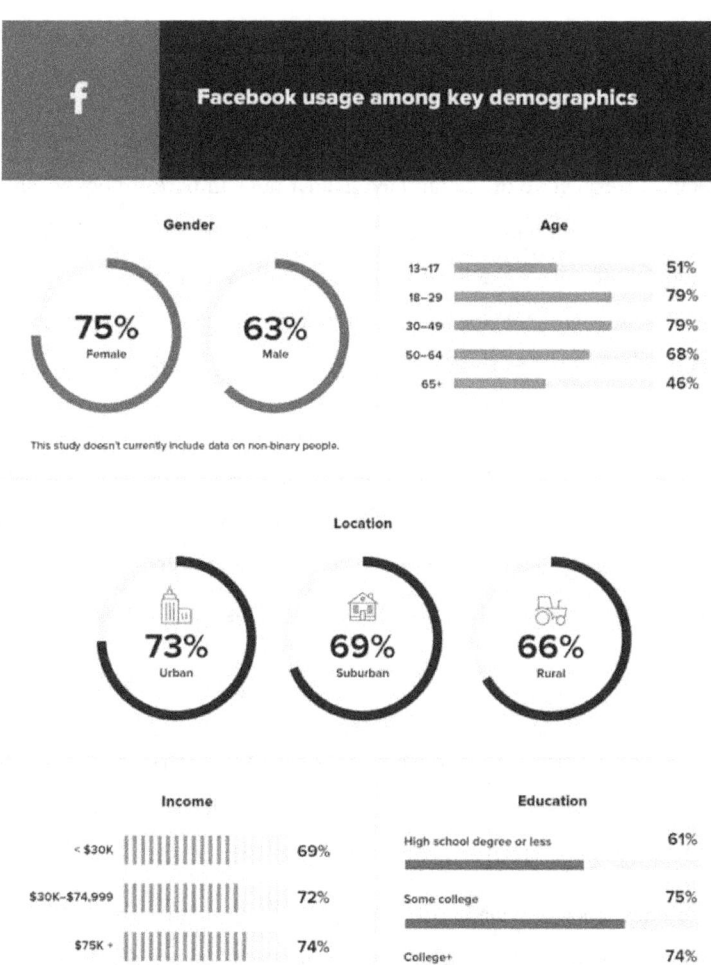

Credit: SproutSocial **and** PewResearch

Of around 190 million users[3] of Facebook in the United States, the majority are aged between 18 and 64. That is a large coverage! The majority of the iGenerations and some of the Millenials are not quite active on this platform. This relatively has led to an increase in their usage on TikTok, Instagram, and YouTube, which is the leading social media platform. So, ideally, if you will be

---

[3] Source: SproutSocial

targeting young age groups (younger than 18 years old), Facebook might not be the best platform for you to promote your business but it will, to a fair level, perform well. You could switch to other platforms that have a high number of teen users.

In the US, 75% of females and 68% of males use Facebook. These statistics show that your campaign will be quite effective irrespective of the targeted gender but can perform better when the female is targeted. However, have it in mind that a good number of adults are using this social media platform and you might want to consider that when selecting the platform or targeting your content and ad. It wouldn't be wise to ignore that the baby boomers also make up a good percentage of the population on this social media platform and can be a good place to market your product and services to them.

As for their residential regions, 73% are said to live in urban areas, 68% in suburban areas, and 66% in rural areas. These numbers give assurance that your campaign will perform well when targeted to people living in any of the regions. When your prospective customers are based in urban areas, you are more likely to have a better target scope considering the other stratification factors.

Any business considering the level of education as a criterion for business promotion can relaxingly use Facebook as a marketing platform. About 61% of people with high school education or less use Facebook, while 75% of those with some college education use the platform also. About 74% of those with more than college education use the platform.

For businesses looking to selling expensive wares like real estate, automobiles, and the likes, Facebook is your best bet. This is because 74% of those making over $75,000 are Facebook users and 72% of those making between $30,000 and $75,000 uses the same. Businesses offering low-cost service or selling low-cost goods can also sell well using this platform.

If you analyze and find out that Facebook is ideal for your business, you have to open a Facebook page for that business. For those new to this, you don't have to open a new Facebook account to create a Facebook page. You can use your existing account and create a page from there. You will find this option when exploring Facebook options.

Take your time to create a custom cover page and you can upload your business logo as the page's profile picture. If you have neither of these, I recommend that you have a graphic designer do your logo for you. You can use DIY design platforms like Canva to design your cover page. Your about page should also be duly updated. Write a short description that will show your audience that you care about them. Complete business info, overview, and others. There are lots of articles online that can guide you in writing something professional.

Once your Page has up to 25 likes, you should customize your page's URL. You should customize it in such a way that it is easy to find and share. It should be something like this; "facebook.com/businessname". Make the name unique and if possible, the same with the username you use on other social media platforms. Simply, use a unique name on all platforms. Share your link on all possible platforms to increase your audience. Another good thing is to pay bloggers to create content about your business and add your link to it to increase your page likes. Embed your page on your website too so that visitors can directly like your page from your website.

When compared to other Facebook posts, videos perform better than other posts type. Videos give room to meaningful interactions that will engage people to watch, share, and comment. This is a 'yippee' moment for those whose businesses are video-oriented. Based on a research made by BuzzSumo, videos of about 3 minutes to 3 minutes 20 seconds in length have the most engagements. So, you might want to consider making your videos within that length but make sure every minute is worth your audience's time.

Facebook is mostly accessed by mobile phone users; hence you should have them in mind when you are creating your content. For posts with pictures, you should consider using a square picture to be able to serve those using laptops and desktop computers too. Also, if you are considering young age groups, you can use a vertical picture for your posts as most of them are mobile phone users.

Also, texts that are up to 50 characters have the best engagement. It would be good if you can squeeze all you want to say into this space. Make it short and simple, not forgetting to make it catchy too.

When linking back to your website, it would be good if you include Facebook pixels on your website to track visits made to your website from Facebook. This will help you optimize your ads and remarket to visitors that have taken some actions on the website. You can ask your developer to include this for you or find out how to do this yourself if you designed your website yourself. It's not hard. It's more of a copy-and-paste thing.

YouTube

YouTube is the largest social media platform presently. Every day, people watch over 1 billion hours of YouTube videos. This statistic is more than the combined record of Facebook and Netflix. With it being the second most visited website after Google, YouTube has a lot of users that are heavy consumers of the platform. Then we can understand why Facebook video ad has more engagement than other content types. People love to get entertained by watching videos!

Credit: SproutSocial **and** PewResearch

From the statistics, 90% of people aged between 18 to 24 years old in the US use YouTube. Exceeding this statistic by 3% are those aged from 25 to 30 years old. One can reason this with 70% of YouTube visits which are from mobile devices as this age group is heavy users of this communication gadget. A very large percentage of adults of no less than 70% are also seen to be users of this platform. This can be a good medium for business promotion when targeting those from 18 to 64 years of age. However, those below 65 years of age are few on this platform as just 38% of them are active users.

With 78% of men and 68% of women using YouTube, one can easily judge that an ad campaign aimed at men will have a better scope on this platform. However, it might be dependent on your target age group. If regional information is to be included, those living in urban areas might have better reach than those in other regions. Thought this does not mean that contents targeted at those in other regions will not perform well as their statistics are also impressive. Also, a good percentage of people with over $75,000 of income uses YouTube. You can be assured that whatever it is you are selling will have a reasonable percentage of people that can afford it.

To sign up for YouTube, you need to create a Gmail account. You should use your business name in creating it. When done, use it to sign up for your business' YouTube account. Once done, customize your business information. A personalized link that people can use to your YouTube channel will be given to you. Customize your channel appropriately and add your YouTube channel art which is very much like Facebook's cover page. Also, upload your business logo as your profile picture. Fill out your business information appropriately, listing your service and other information.

To create your video, you should use a high-quality camera in making your recordings and also make proper editing with a nice background song (recommended). Before you make your video, know what you want and how you want your video to turn out even before you start. You can check competitors' videos to draw inspiration. You can make a video with your mobile phone – if the camera is good, and hire the service of a video editor to include a nice feel to it. You can alternatively get a free or cheap video editor and do the editing yourself.

To get an audience for your YouTube channel, you will need to feature your YouTube channel and videos on other social accounts that you use. It is advisable to have another social media platform(s) that you promote your business on before launching a YouTube site. Alternatively, you can feature your channel link or your videos on blogs that post content related to your business.

There are YouTubers that you can make deals with also. These people have a large number of followers. They can mention your channel or product on their YouTube channel, causing a respective increase in subscribers and sales for you. You might agree on paying them per referral or settle for a one-time payment. Before you use YouTubers to promote your channel, you should have uploaded a few engaging videos on your channel so that your visitors will be interested in your channel after visiting.

Likewise, you can embed your video on your website but advisably not on the home page to increase loading speed. You might embed it in your 'Our story' section of the page. And of course, the video should tell your business story which should be similar to its transcript on the same page.

When your YouTube followers have increased quite well (above 1000 followers), you are qualified to monetize your content. This is another super-cool way to make money on this platform. For engaging videos, e.g videos with DIY content, you can switch on monetizing with an ad for such content. But contents that are emotional or are purely product ad, it is advisable that you switch off monetizing for such. You can go to *YouTube Studio* to switch this on or off.

TikTok

Of all the social media platforms discussed here, TikTok is the newest. It is embraced mostly by people from age 16 to 24 years. TikTok is a fun platform and extremely not a 'let's be serious' platform. With over 33 million downloads, it became the most downloaded app in Apple App Store. In the US, it is seen to have been downloaded over 124 million times, making it the third-highest after India and China.

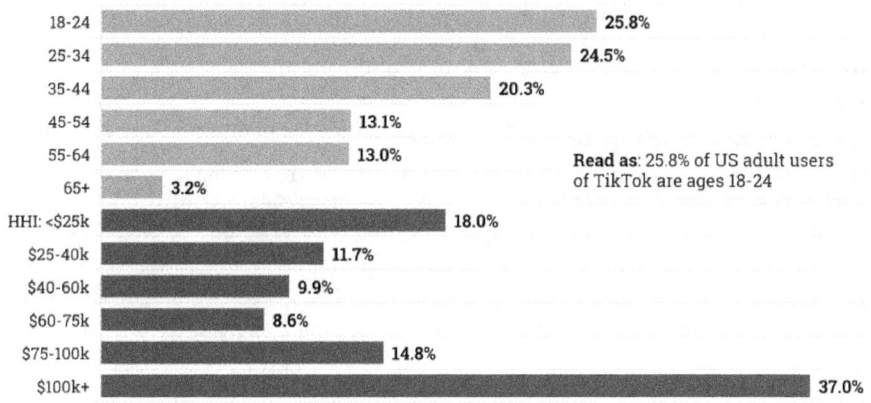

Credit: **Marketing Charts**

TikTok users are seen to make up over 50% of those aged 18 to 34. There is also about 25% of US users that are aged 45 to 64 years. From this, we can deduce that majority of the users are young aged and a significantly increasing number of adults. Those who earn over $45,000 are seen to make up a significantly large number of users.

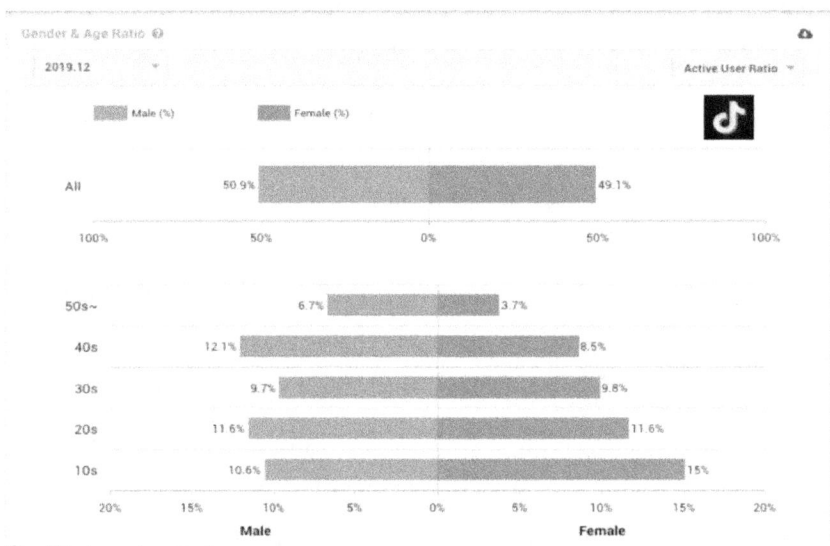

Credit: **App Ape Lab**

Interestingly, the number of female users outnumber male users of the TikTok app in ratio 2:1. Hence, if you are looking to target teenage girls, this platform is perfect for it. For businesses looking to sell fashion wears or some other trendy tings, this platform is good for you to advertise your business too.

You have to be creative to use the platform. You should study the platform before you start creating content to know what type of content is ideal. You have 15 seconds to make your video with music tracks accompanying it. Generally, humorous contents are the most embraced content on TikTok.

You need to download the app on your mobile device to create an account to use the platform. Use your business name to create a username then onward to your first post. Getting followers might be tricky on TikTok without following anyone at first but it is doable.

The very first approach is for you to join trending challenges using the challenge hashtag when posting your video. However, not all the challenges are suitable for businesses but you can find a way to make the video business-related. Here's a demand for your creativity. Sometimes, you might not just think of something exciting enough, ask your friends for suggestions. Something will pop up. Ensure your video is fascinating enough for people to check it out and as a result, follow you.

Also, cross-promotion highly works. If you have a twitter account for your business, for instance, you can promote your TikTok videos on your account. However, attach a link to your shared videos that will lead your audience to your TikTok account and follow you.

You can pay influencers on TikTok to promote your video and attach a link to your page too. They can mention you or use a hashtag you are using too. You can get them to participate in your challenge too. Yes, you can create your hashtag challenge! Creating a challenge is a very good way to have a lot of followers on TikTok. You can discuss with friends to brainstorm a challenge that will be easy to do and will fascinate others. Launch the challenge with your own simple and catchy hashtag and pay influencers to participate in the challenge, encouraging their followers to do the same. In a short period, you will have a significant increase in your followership.

I will say again that you should experiment with TikTok well, even after your first few videos. See what others are posting, what filter they are using, and how you can personalize these ideas to make original content. Posting original content is very essential to getting more followers.

However, make it often to remain relevant and keep your account active. The more the exciting videos you have, the more likely someone who is checking out your profile will follow you.

Quora

For a question and answer platform that has been in existence over 10 years, its 300 million active users, of which 35% of Americans are a part of, is quite applaudable. Quora is increasing in popularity and can be overwhelming for people who don't like to write. You ask and answer questions on this platform.

Males are the most users of this platform as they make up 57% of users. Also, about two-third of Quora's visitors use smartphones and comprise of users that are over 18 years old. So, it might be a bad stop for those targeting teenagers. It would be good to also mention that the most popular topic on this platform is technology. If you are trying to sell a tech product, Quora might then be an option. This shouldn't discourage other businesses as 'Business' is the next most popular question on this website.

Also, it would be good to bear in mind that users of this platform are quite educated. College degree owners are 65% of the users with 28% having graduate degrees. Also, the majority of the users, of about 55%, earn above $100,000 annually.

Creating an account is quite straightforward with a simple profile at the opening end. All you are to update is a profile picture, a short bio, and a few credentials. Your profile can be fully updated in 10 minutes and off you are to start answering questions. Unlike other social media platforms where you will fill in your business profile, you have to fill personal details including your picture. You can then add your Role and your business name as your job credentials (CEO at XYZ Inc. is an example).

As Quora is more like a blog you don't own, be prepared to write a lot of content. As a business owner, I would advise that you ask zero or very little questions on the platform but answer as many as you can. If you would ask a question, ensure that it doesn't in any way arise suspicion about your competency in your industry. But answering questions will prove your competency in your domain.

You have to follow relevant topics and add topics related to your business in the "Knows About" section of your profile to receive questions you can answer. The more people read your answer, the more likely they are to follow you. Even if a question has been answered by someone else, you can still include yours but ensure it's a better answer to earn upvotes and stay on top.

When answering questions, don't market your product – not directly. Just give a sincere answer to the question. However, in between your answers, there might be chances for you to mention your product or service. You can create hyperlinks within your answer or after it. But ensure your content will raise the curiosity of your readers to check out the link. This might be a bit tricky as you have to answer the question sufficiently and refer them to the link at the same time. However, this is possible and has been what most business owners on Quora do.

Highly upvoted answers are fairly long and with pictures. So, if you are writing an answer, you might want to add attractive pictures that are naturally taken. Not super-edited ones. That will catch the attention of your audience. Also, reply to comments and answer people's questions where necessary. It will be important to mention that you should ignore unpleasant comments and reply to those that matter.

Pinterest

Pinterest is an image-sharing social network that has proved to be widely used in the US with over 90 million monthly active users. It is ranked in the United States as the fourth most popular social media platform. It is being used widely to find ideas for hobbies and interests. Likewise, it is used to find inspiration and motivation where necessary. People are embracing this website as it contains endless collections of pictures, gifs, and videos.

A business looking to promote goods or services on this business should be one that can easily communicate it through visualization. Businesses into event planning, home décor, photography, bakery, and many others are the ones that will easily thrive well on this social media platform. What's good about this platform is that about 75% of users claim that they are quite interested in new products and that they use this social media to get shopping ideas[4]. You can hence say that

---

[4] Source: Hootsuite

there is a high possibility of selling your products or services when using this platform. Even app developers have a place there!

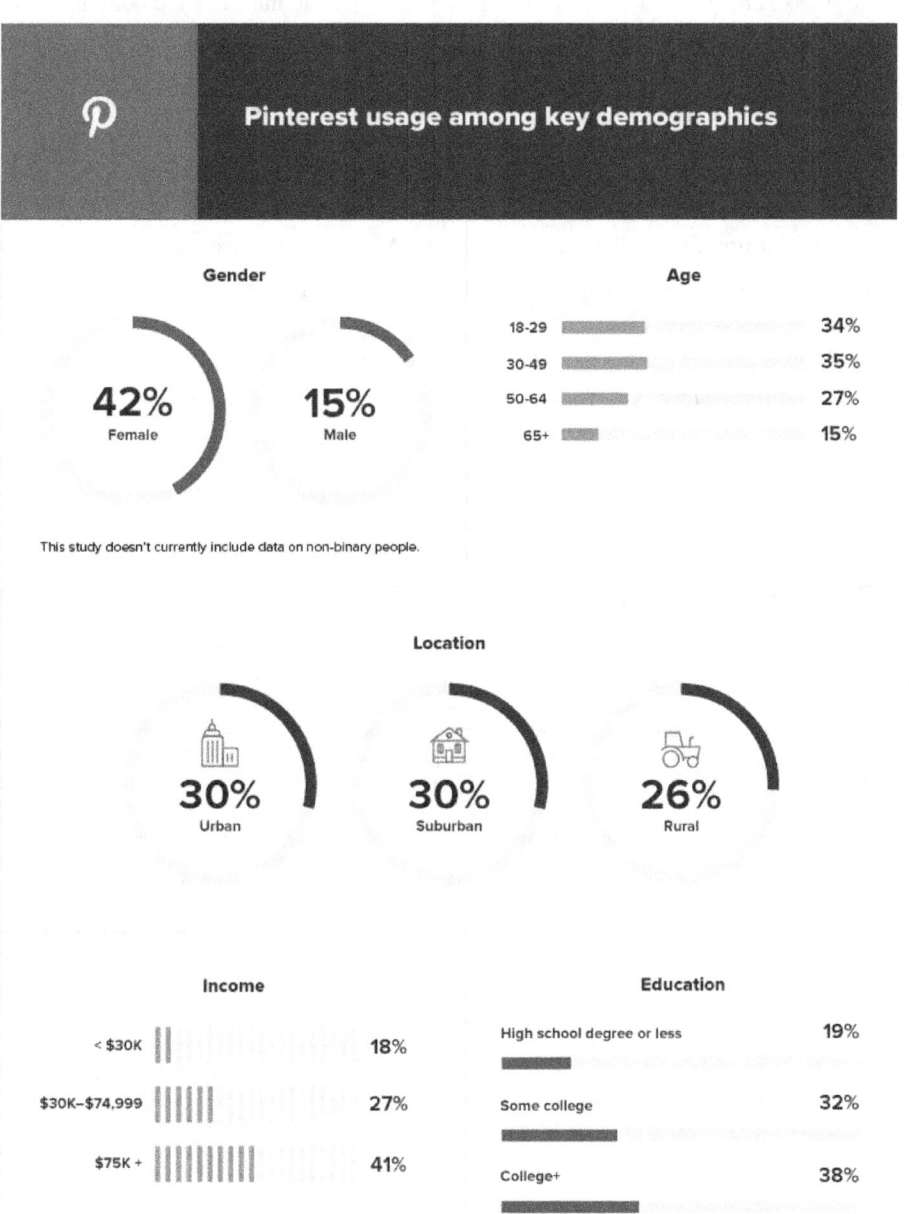

Credit: SproutSocial **and** PewResearch

The demography statistics chart above indicates that 42% of American women use Pinterest while 15% of men use the same platform. This variation is quite large and indicates the dominance of women's presence on the social media website. For those targeting men too, this platform is worth exploring especially if you are targeting the international market.

About 35% of those within the age group of 18 years to 49 years are seen to be interested users. This number is low but usable. Hence, if your target is within this age range, then you might consider using this platform for your business promotion. Also, 27% of those aged 50 to 64 years and 15% of those aged above 65 years are seen to be users of Pinterest.

To get started on Pinterest, you create an account on **pinterest.com/business/create** and then fill all necessary forms appropriately. Afterward, complete your profile setting not forgetting to upload a cover page too. Also, link other social media platforms that you promote your business on. It is advantageous if you do so. Use the claim option to allow you to monitor your website analytics.

After all necessary settings, create a board. This board is more like the name you are giving to a collection of pins – related pictures, gifs, or and videos. Ensure that it is a very possible search keyword. If you are a photographer looking to make compilations of photographs you took for people on their birthdays, you can name the board "Birthday Pictures" or something related. You can make as many boards as possible, so don't worry about not generalizing the name of all your pictures. Ensure you upload a cover photo that fits the board too.

The next thing is for you to create pins. When you click the plus sign located in the upper right corner of your homepage, you can add pictures, gifs, videos, or text on this website with their details and links that correspond to the content's destination. You can pin pictures from your business website, for instance, including the relevant details and link to it. Ensure that the pins are on the right board.

As about 85% of users on Pinterest are mobile phone users, you might want to consider vertical imagery. Also, note that you should go for the highest pictures you can get. Also, be descriptive along with uploading your picture. Don't forget to add a catchy headline too. Ensure that you pin contents regularly – like once in a day, to reach a wider target audience. Videos too should be between 30 to 90 seconds in length –no more. You can share some TikTok videos on the platform too if you are using TikTok for promotion. But ensure it educates and adds a link back to your TikTok video source to potentially increase your TikTok followers.

Mind you, on this website, you can start posting your goods after a while. You upload a picture or short video of your product and attach a price tag. This appears to users looking forward to getting gift items or shop for similar items. However, mind that they can't buy on Pinterest and you have to attach a link to your sales page as appropriate.

You can use influencers on Pinterest too! You don't bother about every other thing but sales when using Pinterest influencers. However, ensure that you have a tangible number of customers. Also, depending on your business, your selection of influencers matters too. An influencer who is majored in targeting members with photography interest cannot be contacted by a bakery business. The promotion might not be effective at the end of the day. Make full-fledged research of any influencer you are considering to use before contacting them. Be convinced they are going to increase your revenue at the end of the day.

Messenger

Facebook Messenger has over 12 billion downloads with around 1.3 billion active users. Initially integrated with the Facebook account, it was later upgraded to be a standalone messaging application. Based on recent researches, marketing on messenger is 70% more effective than email marketing. So, why not use it?!

In the US, 14.7% are aged between 18 to 24 years, 27.3% of users are aged from 25 to 34 years, 21% are aged from 35 to 44 years, while 15.9% of users are aged between 45 to 51 years of age. Adults are more dominant on this social media platform. Users aged between 13 to 17 are also seen to make up 1.7% of the total users.

If you are going to be using messenger as a promotional tool, it would be prudent to add the message button to your business page on Facebook – if you have one. If you choose not to open a Facebook page, for reasons known to you, you might just use the messenger without it.

Using bots is one encouraging way to help your business thrive well on social media. To integrate bots on your social media, you can use several options[5] to build a bot. You can ask a developer to

---

[5] **Check out** Neil Patel's blog

build one for you at an affordable price too. The messenger service is best used with a Facebook account where your Facebook page exists.

Ultimately, this platform is for personal communications and a very good alternative for newsletters. It would be cool if you can integrate a very good Facebook bot to help you answer messages and automatically subscribe people to your newsletter while you are away.

You can upload stories for your customers to see. Stories is a Messenger feature that allows you to upload content for 24 hours. With this in mind, you can upload several contents per day since it will all disappear after 24 hours. Remember, sales are the second option. Educate people and add value to them. That's more welcoming. You can then trust your posts on sales to do well afterward.

Tips and Tricks of SMM

Use Paid Ads

Using a paid ad is a very effective way of reaching your target customers. After building your profile and uploading a few rich posts on your account, it is quite ideal that you use paid ads to quickly increase your reach on a social media platform. All paid ads on social media platforms are quite cheap and can be used even by a startup to increase reach.

When creating ads, you have to target a small cohort of people for high performance. Ensure that the picture or video you are going to be uploading matches the aim of the promotion and that it is catchy enough. Include a catchy heady and a short description too. Be as brief and clear as possible. Also, include a Call-To-Action (CTA) button like a "Buy Now" button where appropriate to create effective and actionable ads.

Boost High-Performing Contents

Contents that have impressively high engagement can be boosted to reach more prospective clients. Using analytics is one very good way to find this out. Analytics is available on all social media accounts especially ones with business accounts. You can from there, determine contents with high engagement.

Test Ads

Testing ads is very important to know the best performing ad that you can spend a larger share of your promotional budget on. When creating paid ads, make several ads while making several changes like changing the target age groups (which should be within your target range), pictures, headings, CTAs, and some other variations. Not all these changes need to be made all at once. You can simply just change the pictures and publish them.

Make the ads run for a few days. Spend about 10% to 30% of your promotional budget on the test ads. Compare their performance using analytics and spend the rest of your budget on the best performing ad. This will save you from a failed promotion.

Post When the Audience is Online

Globally, people have different times they come online due to the variation in time. Hence the need for you to find out your local audience's active time. After you have uploaded a few contents and you have a reasonable number of audience, you can simply check your analytics to find out the time that your audience are active mostly. This feature might not be available for all social media platforms, but you can judge for all using one gotten from a popular website like Facebook.

At this point, you will notice that analytics is quite powerful for social media marketing. It will be quite effective if you use it often to know where improvement needs to be made and when to post content. Ultimately, you'll be able to provide the right value at the right time.

Courtesy is Key

Courtesy in engaging with our audience is quite vital. You need to always maintain a good business face. Even if you get a very annoying review or comment from a customer, reply courteously, showing how sorry you are. Offer to resolve the matter, prompting the customer to update the review after the issue has been resolved.

In building a good relationship with customers, you will need to communicate with them often which will include replying to private messages and comments. And with this in view, you need to be able to handle everything that comes your way calmly and courteously.

Give Discounts and Giveaways

Everyone loves cheap and free things. Once in a while, you can give out some of your products for some little tasks like making referrals or just for the celebration of any sort. It depends on you. You can include this in your ads too. This will, no doubt, increase engagement impressively. Imagine you see an ad of free service for something you need.

Cross-Promote

Cross-promotion is a very effective way of keeping and increasing our followers. It is important to cross-promote content on one of your social media accounts on another social media platform. Showing a video on TikTok and uploading on Pinterest with a link your TikTok account will considerably increase clicks and eventually add more followers to your account.

Invest in a website

If you don't have a website yet, it is advisable to invest in one soon. A website is needed even if you offer a local service. Setting up a website for your business is cheaper than you thought. Try and get one to always create a sales destination for your audience. Also, ensure that the website is mobile-responsive as there is a very high number of mobile phone users.

Always Sell

The ultimate aim is adding value and the next is selling! Don't be scared to sell. You are a business and your audience is aware. Prioritizing the value will make your audience feel safe with buying from you.

Be Patient

Patience is the last and vital ingredient. A lot of people have failed on using social media to promote their business just because they lack patience. You won't have a thousand followers just the next day you open an account. Your audience will grow gradually and like a matrix, increase exponentially with time. The start might be discouraging but the end is definitely worth it. You'll love yourself for it.

CONCLUSION

Now, you have been embedded with the right information that will take your social media marketing strategy to the success zone. You don't have to fear to fail because, with this information and your hard work, you are definitely adding some extra zeros to your business income, all in a short period. You are now set to make powerful content that helps you build a loyal fan base and resultantly, increasing sales.

It's your abracadabra time! Go and create some magic! Get yourself to work if you haven't. Let's give this some practice and see it work. Happy selling!

www.ingramcontent.com/pod-product-compliance
Lightning Source LLC
Chambersburg PA
CBHW050307220526
45465CB00002B/855